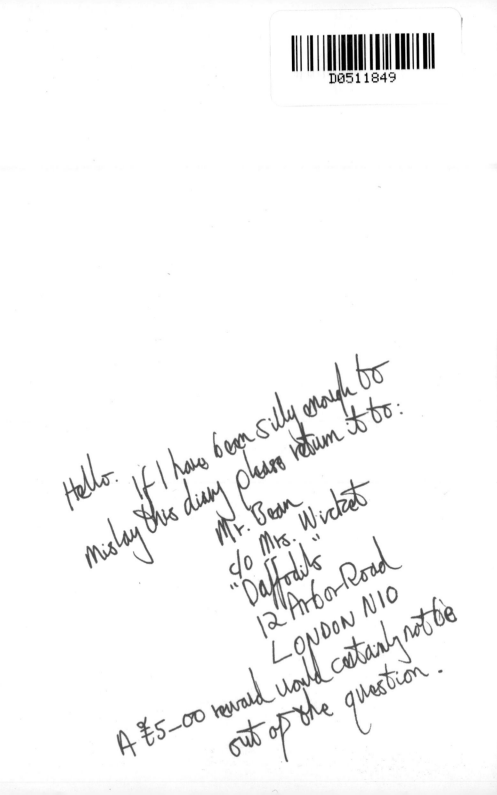

Hello. If I have been silly enough to mislay this diary please return it to:

Mr. Bean
c/o Mrs. Wicket
"Daffodils"
12 Arbor Road
LONDON N10

A £5-00 reward would certainly not be out of the question.

The number of i's on this page is ~~55~~ ~~56~~ ~~57~~ ~~61~~

Published in Great Britain in 2010 by Prion
an imprint of the
Carlton Publishing Group
20 Mortimer Street
London W1T 3JW

10 9 8 7 6 5 4 3 2 1

Designed by Nigel Davis for Titan Studio.
Photography by Paul Forrester.
Printed and bound in Singapore

Front cover photography of Mr Bean courtesy of Stephen F. Morley.
Back cover photography of Mr Bean courtesy of Thames Television.

A catalogue record for this book is available from the British Library.

ISBN 978-1-85375-770-9

my place

Mr. Bean's

HIGHBURY DISTRICT COUNCIL DIARY

So watch it

Compiled for the H.D.C. by
Robin Driscoll and Rowan Atkinson
of the National Diary, Calendar and Phases of the Moon Office
at the Department of National Heritage

P R I O N

HIGHBURY DISTRICT COUNCIL

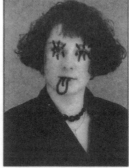

Mayor
Sarah Mahaffy
32 Tongdean Rise,
London N5

Councillor
Nichola Motley
Housing Committee
Broadwaters,
308 Waldergrave Rd,
London N5

Councillor David Inman
Planning Committee
29 Duchland Avenue, London NW8

Councillor Susan Cole
Environment Committee
Flat 3, 21 Downlands Close, London N9

Councillor Chantel Noel
Women's Committee
c/o Highbury Town Hall

Councillor Rod Green
Policy Committee
c/o Highbury Town Hall

Councillor Adrian Sington
Emergency Committee
Church Villas, 15 Dukes Road, London N5

Councillor Elaine Collins
Equal Oportunities Committee
4a George Street, London NW4

Temperature Conversions

°C	°F		°C	°F		°C	°F		°C	°F		°C	°F		°C	°F
-20	-4.0		1	33.8		22	71.6		43	109.4		64	147.2		85	185.0
-19	-2.2		2	35.6		23	73.4		44	111.2		65	149.0		86	186.8
-18	-0.4		3	37.4		24	75.2		45	113.0		66	150.8		87	188.6
-17	1.4		4	39.2		25	77.0		46	114.8		67	152.6		88	190.4
-16	3.2		5	41.0		26	78.8		47	116.6		68	154.4		89	192.2
-15	5.0		6	42.8		27	80.6		48	118.4		69	156.2		90	194.0
-14	6.8		7	44.6		28	82.4		49	120.2		70	158.0		91	195.8
-13	8.6		8	46.4		29	84.2		50	122.0		71	159.8		92	197.6
-12	10.4		9	48.2		30	86.0		51	123.8		72	161.6		93	199.4
-11	12.2		10	50.0		31	87.8		52	125.6		73	163.4		94	201.2
-10	14.0		11	51.8		32	89.6		53	127.4		74	165.2		95	203.0
-9	15.8		12	53.6		33	91.4		54	129.2		75	167.0		96	204.8
-8	17.6		13	55.4		34	93.2		55	131.0		76	168.8		97	206.6
-7	19.4		14	57.2		35	95.0		56	132.8		77	170.6		98	208.4
-6	21.2		15	59.0		36	96.8		57	134.6		78	172.4		99	210.2
-5	23.0		16	60.8		37	98.6		58	136.4		79	174.2		100	212.0
-4	24.8		17	62.6		38	100.4		59	138.2		80	176.0		101	213.8
-3	26.6		18	64.4		39	102.2		60	140.0		81	177.8		102	215.6
-2	28.4		19	66.2		40	104.0		61	141.8		82	179.6		103	217.4
-1	30.2		20	68.0		41	105.8		62	143.6		83	181.4		104	219.2
0	32.0		21	69.8		42	107.6		63	145.4		84	183.2		105	221.0

(handwritten annotations in margins: DEAD, BRR, MMMMM, NICE, PHEW! SIZZLE OUCH!, DEAD, HEE HEE HEE, STUPID)

Conversion Values

Distance
miles to kilometres	1.6093
yards to metres	0.9144
feet to metres	0.3048
inches to millimetres	25.4
inches to centimetres	2.54

Area
square miles to square kilometres	2.59
square miles to hectares	258.99
acres to square metres	4046.86
acres to hectares	0.4047
square yards to square metres	0.8361
square feet to square metres	0.0929
square feet to square centimetres	929.03
square inches to square centimetres	645.16
square inches to square millimetres	6.4516

Volume
cubic yards to cubic metres	0.7646
cubic feet to cubic metres	0.0283
cubic inches to cubic centimetres	16.3871

Capacity
gallons to litres	4.546
quarts to litres	1.137
pints to litres	0.568
gills to litres	0.142

Speed
miles per hour to kilometres per hour	1.6093
feet per second to metres per second	0.3048
feet per minute to metres per second	0.0051
feet per minute to metres per minute	0.3048
inches per second to millimetres per second	25.4
inches per minute to millimetres per second	0.4233
inches per minute to millimetres per minute	2.54

Mass
tons to kilograms	1016.05
tons to tonnes	1.0160
hundredweights to kilograms	50.8023
centals to kilograms	45.3592
quarters to kilograms	12.7006
stones to kilograms	6.3503
pounds to kilograms	0.4536
ounces to grams	28.3495

(handwritten: 10.00 St. Marys)

Mass per Unit Area
tons per square mile to kilograms per square hectare	3.923
pounds per sq. foot to kilograms per sq. metre	4.8824
pounds per sq. inch to grams per sq. centimetre	70.307
ounces per sq. foot to grams per sq. metre	305.152

Mass per Unit Length
tons per mile to kilograms per metre	0.6313
pounds per foot to kilograms per metre	1.4882
pounds per inch to kilograms per metre	17.858
ounces per inch to grams per millimetre	1.1161

Fuel Consumption
gallons per mile to litres per mile	2.825
miles per gallon to kilometres per litre	0.354

Addresses & Telephone Numbers

The Queen
Buckingham Palace (Flat No.?)
London
ENGLAND

Ex directory

Inspector Morse
Oxford Nick
Oxfordshire

999

~~scribbled out~~

Prime Minister
10 Downing Street
London (Weekdays)

071 290 3000

Chequers (W/ends)

0945 482451
(PayPhone — Pub)

Shirley Bassey
On my Wall
In my room
My House
My Street
ENGLAND

081 467 8290

~~Wilkinson~~ KILL KILL
KILL
KILL

GOD
Everywhere   (literally, apparently)

Crematorium
(That place in the trees with
     the chimney)

081 858 5010

Mum
Clapham Cemetery

Grandad
~~152 Grove Road~~
~~London N14~~
(Moved in with Mum)

Shovel Store 071 736 5926

December

Xmas '92

Oooh! Diary for Christmas

3pm   Queen

26 Saturday

↑

Boxing Day?

27 Sunday

↑↑↑

??

Still no sign of Boxing Day

December

28 Monday   Boxing Day

~~Dear Mrs. Queen~~

~~Dear Eliz~~

Dear The Queen

I hope you are well. I am fine. A most peculiar thing
has happened. You may remember that last year Boxing
Day was on the day after Christmas, and most properly so
Why oh why ~~oh why~~

Ever since ~~Alexander that man~~

~~Napoleon~~ Bonaparte was never blown apart ☺

11:00 Como Shop
PILCHARDS

---

29 Tuesday

9.00 Hospital → 291 2777

Tell Doctor: Both ends went in the night
Pilchard?

December

30 Wednesday

12.00 Pie in
12.25 Pie out

31 Thursday

Put the slippery soap
On the slippery slope

NEW YEAR
RESOLUTIONS

1. Become Millionaire
2. Tidy room.
3. Buy other slipper

27. Marriage

Set alarm for 12.00 midnight

January

1 Friday

A brand spanking New Year
Clean and shiny and
sparkling and lovely

1993

GLINT

GLEAM

DURA GLIT

SHIRLEY BASSEY
9.00 Ch4 ???!

10,000 watts

2 Saturday   **3 Sunday**

♪ ◉ △ ◯ + 🔲 = 🔲

January

4 Monday

9.40 Buy new swimming Trunks.

11.00 Try Trunks (Pool)

5 Tuesday

10.00 Report Police Station (re. Trunks
coming off)

(Letter of Apology)   To: St. Bernadette's School for Girls.
Hampstead Road London NW1

Dear ~~Lord~~ Headmistress
Can't apologise enough for awful
incident in front of your young women. ~~Please~~
~~please~~ My ~~~~

4.00 Post Box

6 Wednes

Dear Mr Bean
Rent when I get
home (Sat).

Mrs Wicket

SWINDON BY NIGHT

Mr Bean c/o Mrs Wicket
'Daffodils'
12 Arbor   Rd
London
N10

1ST

7 Thursday

January

8 Friday

4.00 Bottom Problem

9 Saturday

7.45 Keep Fit with
thin woman (ITV)

9.00   20 Press Ups
        20 Sit Ups
        20 Pull Ups
        20 Jump Ups

10 Sunday

9.00 20 Press Ups
     20 Sit Ups
     20 Pull Ups
     20 Jump Ups

That one with the fat
girl 8.00
BBC2

January

11 Monday

9.00 ~~20~~ 10 Press Ups
~~20~~ 10 Sit Ups
~~20~~ 10 Pull Ups
~~20~~ 10 Jump Ups   10.00 Library

Try to get: "Guns Of Navarone"

"His Body Was In Bits"
by Zak Brood   Cliff

"Death Is Frequently Unexpected"
(Z. Brood)

12 Tuesday

9.00 ~~20~~ 4 Press Ups
~~20~~ 4 Sit Ups
~~20~~ 4 Pull Ups
~~20~~ 4 Jump Ups

2.30 Go back and peek
at Librarian
(re. Marriage)

Wobble Dobble Fobble Bobble

January

13 Wednesday

9.00   20 PRESS UPS
         20 SIT UPS
         20 PULL UPS
         20 JUMP UPS

10.00 Peek at Librarian

Irma something

14 Thursday

9.00 20 PRESS UPS
20 SIT UPS
20 PULL UPS
20 JUMP UPS

NO NO
NO
NO NO NO
NO
NO OOOOOOO NO NO

January

15 Friday

9.00 20 Press Ups
20 Sit Ups
20 Pull Ups
20 Jump Ups

HATE HATE

← Mr. Muscles

16 Saturday

17 Sunday

10.30 Visit Mother

←——— 22 along ———→

9 down

MUM

N
W   E
S

January

Ring Irma Gobb
(Library 658 4890)

12.15 Lunch in PARK

12.25 Leave Park (Too much Poo)

4.00 Shops: Carpet Shampoo
Pott Pourri

January

20 Wednesday

9.15 Park

STILL too much Poo in Park

DOG DEVICE

CORK

© Mr. Bean

21 Thursday

Ring Inspector Morse

January

22 Friday

Dear Inspector Morse
There's so much poo in our Park you wouldn't believe it. Can you come and investigate?

I will gladly help you. I have a good ~~set of~~ set of spanners

Mr. Bee Bee Bean ©

---

23 Saturday

That loud one with the beard 6.30 ITV

24 Sunday

Vicar out all day

January

25 Monday

10:00 Library ♡

Take book: Guns of Nav.
2 x Z. Brood

Take out: "Gone with the Wind" (ROMANCE)

"Stand and Deliver"
(Autobiog. of Mollie Saxton, Midwife)

"His blood ran freely" by Zak Brood

26 Tuesday

MR. BEAN

invites you to a Party at
The Park (near-Coin-op Toilets)

DISASTER
IF WET

BRING A SANDWICH
(TWO IF YOU'RE FAT)

Send to
Irma

January

27 Wednesday

4.45 Ring Irma Gobb

Put Cat out ~~of its misery~~

28 Thursday

4.45 Ring Gobb

January

29 Friday

1.30 Wash Spanners

4.45 Get Gobb

---

30 Saturday

Irma Gobb
Has got a Job
In a busy Library
She does her Job
(Does Irma Gobb)
In a library north of Highbury
Irma Gobb
Who's got this Job
Somewhere north of Highbury
Is the same old Irma Gobb
Whose hands are thin and Fibrey

Stadeney Bibley

31 Sunday

February

1 Mon

← Romance?

8.10 Take Irma Gobbo to Pictures

2 Tuesday

Bob a Bob
Joba Bob

Goba Goba Gobble Gobble

February

3 Wednesday

9.00 Ring Gobb

10.00 Ring Gobb

11.00 Ring Gobb

12.00 Ring Gobb

1.00 Ring Gobb

Where is Gobb?

4 Thursday

8.30 Ring Gobb	11.30 Ring Gobb	2.30 Ring Gobb
8.45 Ring Gobb	11.45 Ring Gobb	2.45 Ring Gobb
9.00 Ring Gobb	12.00 Ring Gobb	3.00 Ring Gobb
9.15 Ring Gobb	12.15 Ring Gobb	3.15 Ring Gobb
9.30 Ring Gobb	12.30 Ring Gobb	3.30 Ring Gobb
9.45 Ring Gobb	12.45 Ring Gobb	3.45 Ring Gobb
10.00 Ring Gobb	1.00 Ring Gobb	4.00 Ring Gobb
10.05 Ring Gobb	1.15 Ring Gobb	4.15 Ring Gobb
10.30 Ring Gobb	1.30 Ring Gobb	4.30 Ring Gobb
11.00 Ring Gobb	1.45 Ring Gobb	4.45 Ring Gobb
11.15 Ring Gobb	2.00 Ring Gobb	5.00 Ring Gobb
11.30 Ring Gobb	2.15 Ring Gobb	5.15 Ring Gobb
		6.00 Ring Gobb
		6.15 Ring Gobb
		6.30 Ring Gobb

February

5 Friday

Hate Hate
Hate
HATE Hate
HATE Hate
Hate
Hate Hate
Hate Hate
Hate

HATE

Dear All,
I am having a lovely holiday in Minorca with a *friend* — The weather is delightful and *Giles* a great fun. I hear the weather there is terrible —HOORAY! I will be back at work on the 8th. Lots of love
Irma x

GREETINGS FROM MINORCA

Library
Highbur
Londo
EN

6 Saturday

10.00 Smiths Do-It-All
Either SNIPER RIFLE
   OR ROPE
       SHEATH KNIFE
       STRICHNINE
       MOUSE TRAP?

7 Sunday

February

8 Monday

Hurt
Flay Rap
Slash Songe
Hit
Stab

If I put a bomb under Giles
He will go for miles and miles
And miles and miles and miles
and MILES

†
SILAS
↑ HEAVEN ✗
↓ HELL ✓

9 Tuesday

VENGEANCE

9.30 Crimewatch UK BBC1
(Ideas)

February

10 Wednesday

2.45 Report to
Police Station

Go to bed
ZZZZZZZZZZZZZZZZ
11 Thursday Wake up

2.00—2.10 Sunny

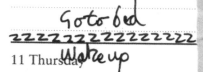

METROPOLITAN POLICE   your ref:
RECEIPT
                          our ref:

Surrendered Goods

1 BRNO .22 AIRRIFLE
1 10" KNIFE
1 SMOKE CANISTOR
3 MOUSE TRAPS
1 lt. ARALDITE
10 m. ROPE

P.C.R.Leavis

The above items have been confiscated pending
a decision by local magistrates

I love P.C. Leavis
xxx

February

12 Friday

Buy ~~Greyhound~~ Fudge   NO
YES ✓✓✓
✓✓✓

13 Saturday

Roses are red
Violets are blue
You were Miss Gobb
And I was Mr. ↰

~~Goo~~ ~~spew~~ ~~the~~ ~~you~~
~~Foo~~ ~~man~~ ~~choo~~
~~Who~~ ~~you~~ True ✓

14 Sunday   St Valentine's Day

No card

Samaritans
071 2367125

10.00 Put Out Bin

February

15 Monday

16 Tuesday

February

17 Wednesday

18 Thursday

February

19 Friday

20 Saturday

21 Sunday

February

22 Monday

....
....
....
....
....
....
....
....
....
....
....
....

23 Tuesday

....
....
....
....
....
....
....
....
....
....
....
....

February

24 Wednesday

FOUND DIARY!!

25 Thursday

1.15 Soup

Hiphip hoozar
Hiphip haha
Yippe Yippee Bippee
Bippee

HAPPINESS

February

26 Fr   ay

No. 3.

Dear Mr Bean,
We haven't met yet but
I have just moved into N°3
down the hall. Enclosed is
your diary which I found
today by the bins in the porch.
I would very much like to
call to make your acquaintance!
and perhaps to pick up the
reward you mentioned on
the first page?!

Man in
N°3. SM

Avoid Man in
No. 3

27 Satur

N.B. Man in No.3

N.B. Man in No.3

March

1 Monday

Shops: Farty Cushion
       False Dung
       Funny hat
       Celery

Those two men in that house 8.30 ITV

AVOID

IN

2 Tuesday

March

3 Wednesday

"Fly Plough"
© Mr. Bean

MAN
No 3

4 Thursday

Where is all this tea coming from?

4.15 Shops: New teapot

March

5 Friday

9.00   N.B. Order Flowers
      for Grandad ✓   ⟵

2.00   Ring Grandma   AAARGH!
                            RING FLORIST
                            RING FLORIST

             Funny Man with wart 10.00 ITV

6 Saturday

9.00 RING FLORIST

7 Sunday

9.00 RING FLORIST

March

8 Monday

⟹ GRANDAD'S 90th BIRTHDAY (QUITE AMAZING REALLY)

RING FLORIST : CHANGE MESSAGE

3pm Grandad Funeral

9 Tuesday

Send off for Shirley Bassey Mug (Large)

to: Shirley's Mug (Large)
P.O. Box 203
Swindon
Wilts. SN43 7PZ

"PORTABLE PHONE"

© Mr. Bean

March

10 Wednesday

3.00pm Ring Irma Cobb — leave funny noises
on Answering Machine
(sobbing?)

11 Thursday

PINK TICKET NO. 77

KEEP IT SAFE

Draw: 27 March

GRAND RAFFLE

In Aid of Police
Benevolent Fund

1st Prize:
A Week
in the Bahamas

2nd Prize:
Dinner for Two at Pizza Hut

March

12 Friday

THE FLOWER

PETAL

MIDDLE BIT

7.30 Botany Club

13 Saturday

LEAF

OTHER LEAF

14 Sunday

GROUND

LITTLE ROOTS

ROOTS

WORM

March

could end up esca...
for a week somewhere.

VIRGO
(Aug 22nd -
Sept. 22nd)
It could be time to retile
that bathroom. You will
receive shattering news
on 27th March, possibly
regarding the number 77.

LIBRA
(Sept 22rd -
Oct 23rd)
All your money worries will
end soon when you get a
big windfall, possibly from
the pools.

GOOD OMEN OR WHAT?

12 DAYS TILL

RAFFLE

16 Tuesday

8.15 Rajpoot Tandoori
(Table for One)

March

17 Wednesday   St Patrick's Day

TEN DAYS

Shops: Loo paper (x6)

Avoid Murphy's Bar

MURPHY'S

PALE STREET

LUKE'S PASSAGE

18 Thursday

NINE DAYS

FRAZZLE
FRAZZLE

JACKET

BAHAMAS

"RAFFLE PRIZE"

© Mr. Bean   (no copycats)

March

19 Friday

EIGHT DAYS

10.30 Building Society
Take all money out
Put no money in

Holiday shopping: Shirts
Socks
Biscuits
Vaseline

Marmalade?

20 Saturday

SEVEN DAYS

Buy holiday shoes

21 Sunday

SIX DAYS

NO shops open
NO shopping
(except Vaseline)

OATH OATH OATH!

Corydalis Lutea

March

22 Monday

FIVE DAYS

4.15 Buy holiday shirts

23 Tues

FOUR DAYS

2 — 4.45
Holiday shopping spree spree spree spree spre

March

3

Buy holiday socks ✓

Ring Building Soc
— No Money

2

Buy holiday celery ✓

If $\triangle + @ + !!! + \text{mw} = \circledast$

and $\pi + \text{❀} - \boxed{\odot} = \triangle$

What is $\boxed{\odot}$?

~~MAD MAD~~
MAD MAD

(4 APRIL)

March

26 Friday

1

FINAL CHECKLIST: MOSQUITO STUFF
FILM
CROCODILE KNIFE
SNAKE GREASE
SPOON

Buy holiday underpants
(both types)

Betty

ooh!

27 Saturday

10.55 Cross Fingers

11.00 RAFFLE
DRAW
St. Andrew's Church
Hall

BLAST OFF

28 Sunday

Travel to
Barbados
on plane

March

29 Monday

Raffle Mystery

THE RAFFLE held in aid of the Police Benevolent Fund was shrouded in mystery last night after the winning ticket number 77 could not be found. The draw had to be held

Arrive in Barbados

Where the blasted heck is that raffle ticket?

30 Tuesday

KILL! SLAY! DAMEUSS!

Barbados

11.00 Start drinking beer

Aster Alpinus

March/April

31 Wednesday

Drink beer all day

Barbados

POL ICE
Station Hebr

Samaritans
2367925

↓ and all night

1 Thursday — April Fool's Day

Barbados

11.45
N° 3.

Dear Mr Bean,
A parcel arrived
for you while you
were out. I have
it with me.

Man in N° 3.
(down hall).

11.15 Man out —
try later

2.10 No Man

4.42 No Man

April

2 Friday

~~Barbados~~

Where oh WHERE is Shirley Bassey mug ?

Ring Swindon.

Try man in No. 3

D. Plumb
Private Investigator
799

7.30 ~~Botany Club~~
Too depressed

3 Saturday

~~Barbados~~

Send back Cliff Richard
mug. GET OUT CLIFF
COME IN Shirley
WHERE ARE YOU??)

4 Sunday

~~Barbados~~

$\boxed{O} = \boxed{} + O$ ✓

Try man
in No. 3.

April

5 Monday

Barbados

Dear Mr. Plumb

I am distraught beyond measure. I have lost a raffle ticket No. 77 and I don't know where to put myself, nor what to do. I have lost all sense of direction and have forgotten how to make tea, even with a tea bag which is so simple, really, isn't it? I last saw the ticket in my hand on March 17th. I don't know where it is. I'm sure I put it somewhere but now somebody called Caroline has gone to Barbados.

6 Tuesday

Barbados

HATE HATE HATE HATE

CAROLINE

Snakes ssss sssss

PLAN VIEW

NO ESCAPE

Ring Samaritans 286 7925 re. Raffle Crisis

April

8.30 Banana

6.00 No Man

N° 3.

Dear Mr Bean,
I know you have been
knocking on my door,
but I have been ignoring
you because there is
no parcel!

APRIL FOOL!!

Man in N° 3
(down hall).

April

9 Friday   Good Friday

6.15 Steal Milk (No. 3)   ~~Barbados~~

Send back Des O'Connor mug.

SEEDS: ~~Pansies~~ NO   Nasturtium ✗
Deadly Nightshade ✓   ⟨7.30 Botany Club⟩
Widow's Misery ✓   Love Lies Bleeding ✓

10 Saturday

~~Barbados~~

10.10 Gorringe's (seeds)
11.00 Plant seeds

8.10 All About Terrapins
(David ~~Attenburgh~~ Borough)
BBC2

11 Sunday   Easter Day

Boiled Egg

Seeds growing

April

Terrapin Budget:

Glass tank	£69 – 95	Seeds Growing
Water	£ 0 – 00	
Filter	£ 15 – 95	
Heater	£ 25 – 50	
Gravel	£ 8 – 00 from shop	
	£ 0 – 00 from next door's drive	
Weed	£ 2 – 50 from shop	
	£ 0 – 00 from next door's garden	
Terrapin	£ 0 – 20p ← CHEAP	

Seeds Growing

April

14 Wednesday

Shirley Bassey mug
arrives HOORAY!

Seeds growing

1.00 Lovely hot steaming mug* of Tea mmmmmmmmmmmmmmmmmm!

15 Thursday

Seeds still growing

10.15 Pet Shop – buy Terrapin

3pm Christening (of Terry)

* Shirley Bassey type, large

April

16 Friday

This makes me so cross

Seeds growing?

17 Saturday

10.00 Check Seeds

Oh, bosoms

18 Sunday

Seeds RUINED
(DOG)

April

19 Monday

9.15 Buy seeds
9.45 Sow seeds

New seeds: Monkey Flower ✓   Red hot poker ✓
Baby's breath (UURGH)   Stinking Helibore ✓

~~Devil-in-a-bush~~ stupid

Plant seeds

---

20 Tuesday   5.45 am Creep out and steal milk

Seeds growing

← RUDDY MOUSE
PRINTS

Ring Samaritans
(keep them talking)

April

21 Wednesday   Queen's Birthday   Ring?

(New) Seeds should
still be growing

"Mousetrap Mk.1"

©Mr.Bean

22 Thursday   5.50am Ssssssssshhhhhh Steal more milk

Wossit
        Grossit
Twissit
        Fossit

Seeds
growing

That really funny one   7.00 Ch.4

23 Friday

SNAP !

10.00 Check seeds

To sum up: 1. Nothing happening
2. No little green bits.
3. No Flowers.
4. No nothing
5. No good.

CUSS CUSS
CUSS CUSS
CUSS

SEED MAN

25,000,000,000,
000,000,000,000,
000,000,000,000,
000,000,000,000,
TONS

24 Saturday

Nº 3.

Dear Mr Bean,
Milk bottles are
frequently stolen
from outside my
door. Can you
throw any light
on the matter?
Man in Nº 3
(down hall).

25 Sunday

He must be really stupid

April

26 Monday

Yabadabadabadabadabadabadabadabadabadabadabadabadabadabadabad OOO!

→ .

27 Tuesday

That grizzly man who was in that old Police programme with Inspector Morse and ran off with the leggy dancer
8.30 BBC1

April/May

If you make a jelly in a teapot
And try to slop it out
It takes about a fortnight
To get it out the spout

Mayday mayday
All around
Ship in fog
Big hooting sound

All that noise and fuss
you make
keep it down
For goodness sake!

Write to Shirley
Bassey re. her
lovely mug

(v.v.v.v.v.v.
v.v.v. important)

May

3 Monday   May Day

"Foot Rest"
© Mr. Bean

4 Tuesday

Give us an S	S	Give us an o	O
Give us a T	T	Give us a .	.
Give us a u	U	Give us a 3	3
Give us a p	P		
Give us an i	I		
Give us a d	D		
Give us an m	M		
Give us an a	A		
Give us an n	N		
Give us an i	I		
Give us an n	N		
Give us an n	N		

What is that spell?

STUPID MAN

IN No. 3

kill kill kill

Yes Yes Yes

May

Highbury District Council
Council Offices
Highbury, London N10

Mr Bean,
c/o Mrs Wickets,
Daffodils.
Room 2, 12 Arbor Road,
London N10

15th May 1993

Dear Mr Bean

Thank you very much for your letter of the 5th May concerning, as you see it, the "outrageous" shape of your toilet.

Unfortunately, the obligations of your local council extend only as far as the provision of sewage facilities in the borough, and we cannot be held responsible for the shape of any individual apparatus. Certainly the shape of the pan you describe (your drawings are returned herewith) would appear to be traditional.

I was naturally distressed to hear of the effect that this "mad toilet" is having on your mental health. Your nightmares, accompanied, as you claim, by the "banshee howls" akin to the sound of "two enmeshed chainsaws (two-stroke)" would only become the responsibility of the local authority if complaints were received from other tenants at Daffodils. This department has no record of any such correspondence.

I therefore cannot entertain your request for a Community Charge rebate, merely on the basis of the "horrifying scenes" you describe, and the blame which you directly attribute to the curvature of your lavatory.

Yours sincerely

G.M. Nuttall

May

7 Friday

"Man Basher" (re. No.3)   © Mr. Bean

8 Saturday

TEE HEE HEE

9 Sunday

9.15 Rubbish

10.00 More Rubbish

May

? ← (chicken drawing) TON ← CHICKEN SOUP.

10 Monday

Hello Monday you look nice and fresh, but then you're always the first day aren't you?

11 Tuesday

Oh Tuesday goodness me you've come along too, how delightful. How do you do?

May

12 Wednesday

Ooops! Gave me a bit of a fright there Wednesday although "" I should have expected you, I know, because you always bowl up on Day 3. Sit down, do.

I've got some bitter lemon if you'd like some but nothing alcoholic I'm afraid (burp)

Oh, and Wednesday

13 Thursday

this is Thursday.

Oh, you've met, I'm sorry. You met last week?

How interesting!

Silly me.

May

14 Friday

FRIDAY where have you been?

I've been so anxious. You're always so late, you naughty boy, the week's nearly over. Honestly.

15 Saturday

Brr Brr. Brr Brr.
Ting.
Hello? Yes, Mr Beam here. Can you not make it Saturday? But it's the sixth day, and you're expected. Oh tish pish posh.

16 Sunday

The Lord's Day

(not my responsibility)

May

17 Monday

THE GROCER (Caught Unawares)

Blancmange
Stonehenge

Nothing rhymes with Orange
Except perhaps Lozenge.

18 Tuesday

3.

© Mr. Bean

CARROT

May

19 Wednesday   8.15 Get up.

Ring Irma Gobb

Join Poetry Class 7.30
(Ms. Rosemary
Haseburg)

10.30 Go to bed

20 Thursday   8.15 Get up

If I had a newt
I'd have a pursuit.

Poetry research: Buy daffodils
Ring T.S. Eliot

9.30 Go to bed

May

21 Friday

Eliot N, 25 Dunleary Drive, N17   081 801
Eliot N.P.J, 35a Henderson St, SE10   081 293
Eliot N.T, 16 Cudworth Gdns W12   081 740 0
Eliot O.C, 8 Nightingale Cres, SE18   081 316 0
Eliot P.F, 3 Hawthorn Mews,
     Hawthorn St, SW12   081 675
Eliot P.R, 253 St Winifrides St, NW11   081 45
Eliot S.T, 68 Whoriton St, W10   081 956
Eliot T, 43 Yately Walk,
     Brookside Est, E17   081 521
Eliot T.A, 92 Chippendale Rd, W5   081 997
Eliot T.D, 57 Barling Gdns, SE7   081 85
Eliot T.J, 17 Everard St, SE24   071 37
Eliot T.J, 101 Driscoll Drive, N20   081 4
Eliot T.P, 5 Atkinson Lane, SW18
Eliot T.R, 22a Green Gdns, E14
Eliot A, 95 Davies Rd
Eliot A.R, Ro

T.S. Eliot ex-directory?.

10.30 Go to bed (Boring)

22 Saturday   9.30 Get up   (Yippee!)

10.30 Go to bed.

23 Sunday   Don't get up

If I haven't got up then I won't have to go to bed. HOORAY!

May

24 Monday

Ring Irma Gobb
And keep it clean
If you get
Answer machine.

Shirley Bassey in Pro-Am Golf   8.00 BBC2

25 Tuesday

DAM DAM DAM DAM DAM
DAM DAM DAM DAM DAM
DAM DAM DAM
DAM

May

26 Wednesday

Poem: ATTENTION MICE

You'd better watch out
Cos if I see you about
You're going to end up in my mincer
Then, no mucking about
I'll scrape you all out
And do the same thing to your sister

7.30 Poetry Class

27 Thursday

"MOUSETRAP MK.2"

© Mr. Bean

May

28 Friday

9.00 Buy Fish

Leave out all day

29 Saturday

Leave out all day

30 Sunday

← Really smelly now

3.

Tee hee hee

31 Monday

Up at nine
Out by ten
Drive to town
Drive home again

Those two men in that house 8.00 ITV

1 Tuesday

HOUSEFLY

FILTH

"HOUSE FLY TRAP"

© Mr Bean

June

2 Wednesday

Picnic shopping : Tea Bag
                   Lettuce
                   Sticklebacks in Brine

1.oo Picnic in Park.

                                      Cilla Black
                                      Has a lack
                            (but) Shirley Wifey
                                   → Is a cuddly girley
7.30 Poetry Class   (Bassey)

3 Thursday

Don't do ANYTHING today AT
                              ALL

                    except go to the toilet

CRASH!

3.

4 Friday

Oh Lord who giveth and
taketh away, taketh away Terry
and put him in a nice big tank
in heaven and remember to feed
him because I forgot

Amen.

Terry (the Terrapin) R.I.P.

5 Saturday

Give Terry's tank, water,
weeds, and gravel away
to somebody —
⤷ oxfam?

HELP FEED STARVING TERRAPINS ALL OVER THE WORLD

6 Sunday

Help on it's way

WHOOSH HELP

OFF

June

7 Monday

There's a poetry test
I'm sure to pass
In Ms Rosemary Roseberry's
Poetry class
She's given us the title
"A Goddess Sublime"
Which will take no time
For the Prince of Rhyme (to do)

8 Tuesday

9.45 Turn in

POETIC LICENCE
ALL
CATEGORIES
EXPIRES: 7 JUNE 1994
Mr BEAN   MALE

<u>A GODDESS SUBLIME</u>   by Mr. Bean

If there's anything in the world
That I would like to be
It's Shirley Bassey's microphone
So she could sing to me

I know she sings to everyone
When they come to hear her
But front row seats cost fifteen quid
And I would be much nearer.

Another thing that strikes me   7.30 Poetry Class

About being up that close

Is that I could smell her perfume
And see right up her nose*

I know microphones get dribbled on
But so what, what the hell?
It is a perk of the job when it's Shirley's gob
And I'd get in free as well!

* N.B. Check with Ms. Hosebury — close & nose rhyme

June

Poo-ee!

Ring Samaritans
re drains

12 Saturday

13 Sunday

11.15 Forget it

Get up early tomorrow

June

14 Monday

11.10 Give blood

15 Tuesday

Dear ~~Council~~
~~Nurse Gibbey,~~

Wash out
Jam Jar

Dear Blood Man/Woman

I would like to become a blood donor and enclose, for your perusal,

June

16 Wednesday

Highbury Royal Infirmary
Highbury, London N10

re: 16 June
from: Highbury Royal Infirmary

Dear Mr Bean

Although we are pleased that you have decided to become a
blood donor, I'm afraid that we cannot accept donations by
post. We have disposed of your blood in accordance with the
conditions of the Medicines Act 1709, and your jam jar is
returned herewith.

Perhaps you would like to give blood when a mobile unit visits
your area? If you would like further information, please see
your doctor.

17 Thursday

Perhaps you will be seeing your doctor anyway?

Yours sincerely

Jose Manteras

Jose Manteras
Doctor

June

18 Friday

"GRISTLE MASTER"

© Mr. Bean

---

19 Saturday

Shops: Loaf
Butter
Egg (x2)
Spindle
Grommet

20 Sunday

June

21 Monday

Tipula Maxima

6.00 Lance Boil

22 Tuesday

9.15 Lance Boil

6.15 Ring Lance Boil

7.45 Entymology Club
↳ What is Entymology?

CRASH!

23 Wednesday

Morning: Go to Library

...nas -uus f. *integer*: see ENTIRE]
...e /ɪnˈtaɪt(ə)l/ *v.tr.* **1 a** (usu. foll. by *to*) give (a person etc.) a just claim. **b** (foll. by *to* + infin.) give (a person etc.) a right. **2 a** give (a book etc.) the title of. **b** *archaic* give (a person) the title of (*entitled him sultan*). ▢▢ **entitlement** *n.* [ME f. AF *entitler*, OF *entiteler* f. LL *intitulare* (as IN-², TITLE)]
entity /ˈentɪtɪ/ *n.* (*pl.* -ies) **1 a** thing with distinct existence, as opposed to a quality or relation. **2 a** thing's existence regarded distinctly. ▢▢ **entitative** /-tətɪv/ *adj.* [F *entité* or med.L *entitas* f. LL *ens* being]
ento- /ˈentəʊ/ *comb. form* within. [Gk *entos* within]
entomb /ɪnˈtuːm/ *v.tr.* **1** place in or as in a tomb. **2** serve as a tomb for. ▢▢ **entombment** *n.* [OF *entomber* (as EN-¹, TOMB)]
entomo- /ˈentəməʊ/ *comb. form* insect. [Gk *entomos* cut up (in neut. = INSECT) f. EN-² + *temnō* cut]
entomology /ˌentəˈmɒlədʒɪ/ *n.* the study of the forms and behaviour of insects. ▢▢ **entomological** /-məˈlɒdʒɪk(ə)l/ *adj.* **entomologist** *n.* [F *entomologie* or mod.L *entomologia* (as ENTOMO-, -LOGY)]

← BINGO!

24 Thursday

ANGRY IRMA

TEE HEE HEE HEE HEE

June

25 Friday

11.00 MFI (Cupboard – self assembly)

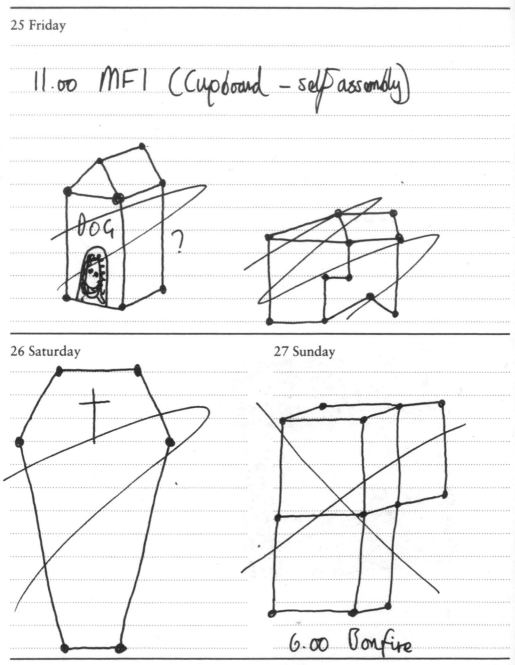

26 Saturday

27 Sunday

6.00 Bonfire

June

CRASH!

28 Monday

Oh what a horrible morning oh what a horrible day
I've got a horrible feeling that people just get in my way

but only ONCE

and then it's CURTAINS

29 Tuesday

for them

Heh heh heh heh heh
heh heh

Yesterday up on the stairs
I caught a man unawares

I gave him a fright again today
By taking both his ears away

(You should have seen him)

7.45 Entymology Club
(Spelling 10/10)

June/July

30 Wednesday

6.00 News (BBC) De de dom de de domm de de dum dum dum dum dos dos dos dum dum dos dos dum dowmmmm... ...This is the Six O'clock News from the BBC with thingummy jig and whats her face...... de de domm de de dumm.

1 Thursday

Tenebrio Molitor

10.00 News at Ten (ITV)
(Pay attention)

July

2 Friday

Shops: Shake 'n Vac

→ 12.00 Clean Jacket (Tweed)

3 Saturday

9.20 Go out
10.04 Come in
10.24 Go out again
12.10 Come in again
1.45 Go out again
2.05 Come in again
2.55 Go out again.
2.56 Come in again
2.57 Go out again
4.50 Come in again
6.05 Go out again
6.43 Forget to come in again
7.00 Miss Programme
7.28 Eventually come in again

4 Sunday

CANCELLED

July

5 Monday

Ring Irma Gobb?

No, can't be bothered.

I would very much like to go to the moon, even though I don't like travel, as a rule. No language problems, and no crowding.

6 Tuesday

Also, no air.

GASP GASP
GASP

9.10 Over the moon about something ➝ ♀

7.45 Entymology Club   lots of creepy crawlies

July

7 Wednesday

Young people with ~~funny~~ horrible accents 5.40 BBC1

8 Thursday

Shopping (to service car):

GREASE
OIL
Egg WHISK
Filter
Coffee
G-Clutches
Spotting spigot

Fairy liquid
Alarm clock ?
Bottle (don't lose it)

July

CRASH!

CHANGING THE OIL

BEFORE

AFTER

TOUCH-UP PAINTWORK

CHANGE BULB
IN BOOT

ALL DONE!

Entymology Club 7.45

July

14 Wednesday

OLD Getting dressed procedure: First Shirt
then Socks
then Underpants
then Trousers
then Shoes
then Tie
then Belt
BORING then Jacket

15 Thursday

NEW Getting dressed procedure:

First Shirt
then Jacket
then Tie

First Shoes
then Socks

First Trousers
stupid then Undies
Impossible
→ stupid
→ barmy

First Belt
then Tie
then Shoes
then Leave House
Too rude
then Jail

First
then Undies
then Jacket
Tie
Madmad
Mad

CRASH!

16 Friday

10.45 Library   Return   "Gone with the Wind"
                        "Stand and Deliver"

             Get out   "Insects of Yesteryear" by E. Dalton

                    "The Land of Gore" by Zak Brood
                    "Limb from Limb" by Zak Brood
                           (Parts 1 & 2)

                    "Are you bleeding comfortably?"
                                 (Z. Brood)

<u>also</u> Ask Gobb to Pictures

---

17 Saturday

6.10 HORROR FILM

18 Sunday

10.15 Vicar (Exorcism)

Sleep with light on

July

19 Monday

Seek
Professional
Help.

20 Tuesday

North London
Technical College
Highbury, London N10

Mr Bean,   16th July 1993
c/o Mrs Wickets,
Daffodils,
Room 2, 12 Arbor Road,
London N10

Dear Mr Bean

I'm sure that I need not reiterate the horror and revulsion felt by all of
us when you revealed your pressed insect collection. It is inhuman
to murder God's creatures in this way, merely to form a macabre
collection in the pages of your diary.

There has been a unanimous decision taken by our sub-committee
to report your behaviour to the RSPCA, from whom I hope you will
be hearing soon.

You really are a quite revolting man.

Dr. Legge

Dr. Legge
Sec., Entomology Club

July

CRASH!

21 Wednesday

Seek Professional Help re. Nightmares

Can't sleep

22 Thursday

Can't sleep

Clossiana Euphrosyne

July

23 Friday

Smiths Do-It-All : 1 Mirror
: 1 Wooden stake

Sainsburys : 10 lbs Garlic

Sleep with light on

24 Saturday

25 Sunday

8.30 Holy Communion
9.30 Family Service
11am Mattins

Lock door
Sleep with light on

6.30 Evensong
(Attend religiously)

July

26 Monday

Stay in all day

Breathe quietly

...ideo: The Exorcist

SSS SSS SSSSssschhhhhhhhh---

27 Tuesday

SCREAM

Pull myself
together.

July

28 Wednesday

Close my eyes
Up tight and sing
Go away
You big bad thing!
Open them again
And shout

GO AWAY

29 Thursday

NEW
SECURITY
ARRANGEMENTS

GE

July/August

30 Friday

or you'll

6.00 Shirley Bassey
Master Chef

31 Saturday

1 Sunday

A CLOUT!

August

2 Monday

Feeling much better today, thank you.

Shops: Beans
Bread

Long Johns

3 Tuesday

9.45 Mrs. Wicket (Root)

7.15 Burn something
(Mrs. Wicket?)

August

4 Wednesday

Significant disturbances.

Beans for dinner
Beans for tea
Oh windy Bean
Oh windy me

5 Thursday

Further disturbances (Bottom Dept.)

© Mr. Bean

August

6 Friday 8.30 Take Mini to Man

A. & G. MOTORS

10 Ugly Street, Twickenham
081 851 1590

Dear Mr Bean

I thought you should know, that your mini is
a Dog. We looked at it this morning. and it
is completely clapped. You need a new sub
frame mate and by ends and mounts and
exhaust etc to name but a few. Tires
are as bald as that swimmer bloke. We're
talking a lot of cash. like two or three
hundred also the brown stuffs everywhere
(you been driving fast again !!!!!!!) No I
mean the rust its terrible the car is
really shot. My feet went through the
floor at Sainsburys roundabout, Fred
Flintstone Eat your heart out !!! Come to
the garage and you better say what you
want cos we're going to Rimini Tuesday.

Graham

P.S. My mate thinks you're weird

7 Satur

August

CRASH

9 Monday

"HANDY ASH"

© Mr. Bean

10 Tuesday

12.00 Park

Dear ~~Highbury As~~ Council Man

The state of the park is very outrageous and, in a way, cataclysmic, it is so smelly. I know I may have contributed to the aroma myself recently, because as you may know, I have had my own problems, but the poop is charitable that...

August

'ANTI-DRIP'
© Mr. Bean

11 Wednesday

12 Thursday

"Daffodils"
12 Arbor Rd.
LONDON N10

BEAN ANTI-POOP ASSOCIATION (BAPA)

Dear Resident

    I hope you are well. I am fine. I am writing to ask if, like me, you are sick and tired of too much poop.

Dogs, treat this road, and the park, like a huge toilet, which it isn't. Join 'BAPA' and help me stamp out poop. Any dog owner caught ~~fouling our paths~~ allowing a dog to foul our paths will get a right dressing down, and further abuse. Those responsible for more than one poop will get a punch up the bracket. (We could take it in turns)

If you are interested, please fill in this form, and send it back.

- - - - - - - - - - - - - - - - ✂ - - - - - - - - - - - - - - - -

NAME . . . .
ADDRESS . . . .
. . . .
. . . .

I think your idea is great. Signed .
. . . .

August

13 Friday

9.45 Library (Photocopies). n/f . Too much poop (BAPA)

Ring Samaritans
        re. poop.

14 Saturday

15 Sunday

Do I like Golf?

IN →

August

16 Monday

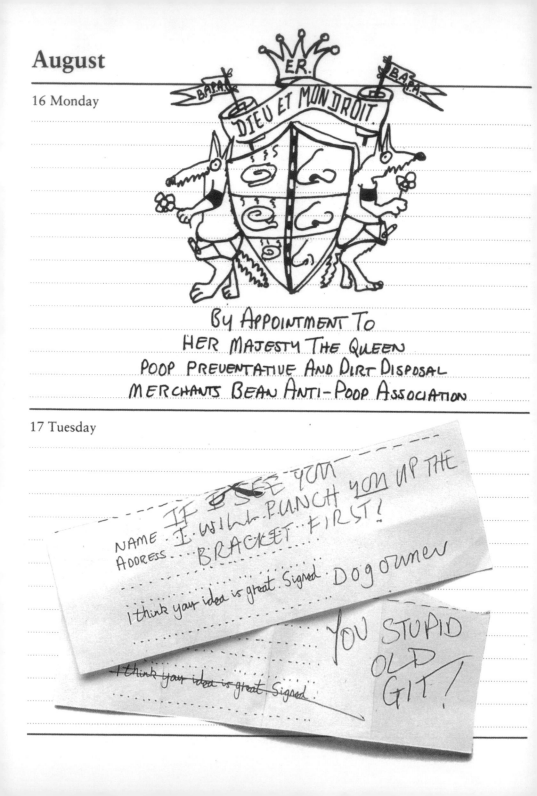

BY APPOINTMENT TO
HER MAJESTY THE QUEEN
POOP PREVENTATIVE AND DIRT DISPOSAL
MERCHANTS BEAN ANTI-POOP ASSOCIATION

17 Tuesday

18 Wedne

CRASH

Benny
...7.A. Arbor...

...pathetic...
...r idea is great. Signed

P. Benny

NAME DONALD DUCK
ADDRESS PLUTO

I think your idea is great. Signed. BOG OFF!

V. R. NUTS.
LOONY BIN

I think your idea is great. Signed
Neville Chamberlain

You should be locked up
I think your idea is great. Signed Frederick

Go it alone

METROPOLITAN POLICE
4, Guildford Street
Highbury
London N10

Dear Mr. Bean

It has been drawn to our attention that you have been circulating letters to the residents in your area of the borough, complaining about the problem of dogs fouling the pavement. This is not a criminal offence in itself, but the blatant incitements to violence which are also contained therein most certainly are.

We received a complaint from a dog owner yesterday, claiming that he was recently attacked by a man answering to your description. After the complainant's pet had made an accidental deposit in the park, the attacker attempted to force the owner's nose into the excreta. This is not the kind of behaviour that upstanding citizens should have to suffer. The hooligan was also carrying a quantity of corks, with one of which he attempted to violate the dog.

If this attacker was yourself, you must appreciate that the Constabulary takes a very dim view of this kind of behaviour: if we hear of any similar incidents, or af any further letters, criminal proceedings will be brought against you.

Yours sincerely

Sgt. Rickers

Sgt. P.R.D. Rickers

CRA

23 Monday

9.00am Commence BAPA Stealth Deterrent Mk. 1

Glue	Tow bar
Soup	Pillow case
Timber 24' x 1½" x 1½"	Electric Fan
Duvet Cover	Bed sheet
Broom handle	Screws
Bread Knife	Nails
	Horse Poop (½ Ton)

24 Tuesday

Fig. 1

The fat man with the long hands 6.30 BBC1

August

Sore throat

I've got to be firmer
with Irma
If she's going to be
A long termer

Nose getting blogged

Nose completely stuffed
Full of snot.

Chemist: Paraffin
Pipe cleaners?

4.00 Unfortunate snot accident (Mrs. Wicket)

27 Friday

Letter of Apology (Mrs. Wicket)

BAPA Detonant: Fig. 2

---

28 Saturday

Construction to continue
apace.

9.00 Bonk bonk bonk

2.30 Tap tap tap tap

8.15 Kersplak kersplak

29 Sunday

7.00 Bang bang bang bang
bang bang bink OWW!
Bang bang bang

August

30 Monday

3'

string

2'6"

2'6"

Cover with
Pillow case

EMPTY
Soup
TIN
(HINGE

31 Tuesday

Soup

BAPA Detergent Fig.3 RUDDER

September

1 Wednesday

MRS. WICKET IN BRIGHTON

10.00 Clear Drive
10.30 DELIVERY OF HORSE POOP

2 Thursday

Morning: Fill Duvet Cover with horse poop.

Recipe Idea: RABBIT STEW
2 PTS. Hot Water
1   Rabbit
1   Plate
1   Knife
1   Fork   Boil, Serve, Eat.

September

3 Friday

Shops: More screws
        Bigger screws

N.B. Need to change Traffic Light sequence, junction
of Arbor Road + New Road

Requirements: Screwdriver
              Pliers
              Mini
              Brain on
              full Alert

---

4 Saturday | 5 Sunday

ARBOR ROAD

N
E
W

R
D.

CONTROL
BOX

- - - - = ESCAPE
          ROUTE

Fig 4 Stealth Lights Plan

Saturday Nights the night
for fighting.
            (Stay in)

September

6 Monday

2-6pm Saw!
Saw!
Saw!

9'

BAPA Fig. 5

Lift
1,500
lbs

25 Forward
knots Speed

N
W — E
S

Looking Good
for Mon 13th

September

8 Wednesday

8.30 Biff Biff Biff Screech

11.am Bang bang bang

BAPA Plan Fig. 6

9 Thursday

½ ton

2.00 Biff Baff Boff

2.30 Bimmer Bimmer

10 F...

N°3.

Mr Bean,
I have not slept
for three nights.
If the banging
does not stop I
will call the police.
Maria. N°3.
(down hall.)

Oh, go away
and sit on a cabbage
(for the rest of your
life)

---

11 Saturday

Dear God
        Oh Lord, who giveth
and taketh away. Giveth me
luck on Monday but taketh me
not away; unless I do something
really awful like forget to
flush the toilet
Yours sincerely

Mr. Bean

P.S. I hope you are well. I am fine.

12 Sunday

11.15 Church (Pray, pray,
            pray)

September

DA-DAAAA!

13 Monday

LAUNCH

→ 25 knots

CUT

14 Tuesday

DUNG-FILLED DUVET

TUM TE TUM TE TUM...

September

15 Wednesday

Highbury Herald September 15 1993

Bizarre man foiled

A HIGHBURY man's attempt to "put the world to rights" was foiled after police received a tip-off that a lime green mini was about to be launched from the roof of WH Smith in New Road.

The owner of the car, a Mr Bean of Arbor Road, Highbury, was first spotted by pedestrians on the street below, who alerted the police.

"The vehicle in question was fitted with a home-made set of wings, rather like a hang-glider, on the roof," said a police spokesman. "The wings upon inspection seem to have been made from an old bed sheet and some lengths of wood. Also in the car we found a bread knife attached to the end of a broom handle, and an electric fan."

Police are puzzled as Bean's possession of ton of horse

Nagging thought (re. my origins)

4.45 Police Station

11.00 Further questioning.

September

17 Friday

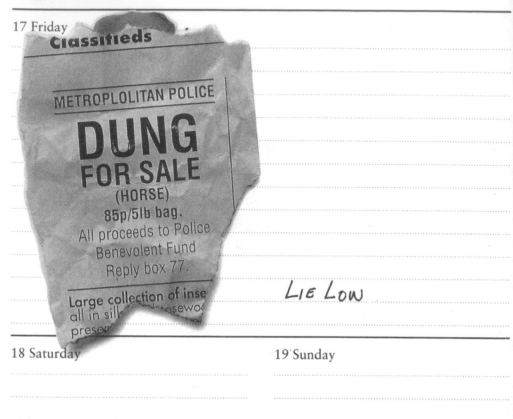

Classifieds

METROPLOLITAN POLICE

DUNG

FOR SALE

(HORSE)

85p/5lb bag.

All proceeds to Police
Benevolent Fund
Reply box 77.

Large collection of inse
all in sil   osewoo
preser

LIE LOW

18 Saturday

LIE LOW

19 Sunday

LIE LOWER

N° 3.

Dear Mr Bean,
I don't believe
your car was stolen
at all. I saw the
horse dung on the
drive, and I think
you are completely
mad.

Man in N° 3.
(down hall)

I've a funny feeling my
birthday was last Wednesday.

21 Tuesday

3.

STINK

© BEAN 1993

September

22 Wednesday

NAME Mr. D. Wilkinson
ADDRESS 23A Cherry Lane
London
N.5.
I think your idea is great. Signed
D. Wilkinson

YIPPEE!!

23 Thursday

9.15 Ring Mr. Wilkinson

4.30 Mr. Wilkinson for tea

Shops: Crumpets   Stodgy cake
       Crusty buns   Lovely cake
       Juicy Cake + other cake
       Big cake
       Small cake

September

24 Friday

NEW IMPROVED
"SNAIL" RULER

© Mr. Bean

J.00 BANK - get £500
for Mr. Wilkinson

---

25 Saturday

10.00 Drive Mr. Wilkinson
to shops

J.15 Mr. Wilkinson's ointment

26 Sunday

10.00 Polish Mr. Wilkinson's
knobs
+ knocker

Mr. Wilkinson borrowing
car this afternoon.

10.00 Car due back

September

27 Monday

WHERE IS MR. WILKINSON?

0AM STAB
CUSS WRETH
DISMEMBER DISEMBOWEL

3.45 Police

WHERE OH WHERE IS MY LOVELY CAR

28 Tuesday

8.40 Catch bus to shops

9.20 Bus

4.30 Smelly bus home again

September

29 Wednesday

Poem: <u>MIND YOUR GRANNY</u>

If there's one thing that's not fetching
It is the sight of someone retching
So at Grandma's please do be extremely careful
If you need to vomit after tea
Then in the toilet you should be
So as not to give your Gran a sticky earful.

Mr. Bean 29 Sept 1993

7.30 Poetry Class

30 Thursday

Possible chorus: Pewky pewky retch retch
Head inside the bowl
Keeping it from Granny
Should be your intended goal.
Tra la

<u>Show to Ms. Rosemary Hoseburn</u>

October

1 Friday

WHERE is my £500 ?

WHERE is my car ?

WHERE is slimy puss-y slimbag Mr. Wilkinson ?

2 Saturday

London Transport
PHOTOCARD

Name of holder
MR/M S
Mr. Bean

Valid for use only by person
shown with a ticket
bearing the same number.

T 5328

I HATE THE BUSSSS

October

4 Monday

20,000 ft

"LEMMING BUSES"

© Mr. Bean

5 Tuesday

Plan: 10.00 Catch bus
10.15 Torture bus
11.00 kill bus

RIP

LONDON BUS

October

6 Wednesday

Shops: Ace
Celery

7.00 Start Bell Ringing

7 Thursday

That revolting couple   ITV (Morning)

9.30 Bell Ringing

8 Friday

1.45am   Bell Ringing

Saturday   Sunday

11.00 More Bell ringing

No 3.

Dear Mr Bean,
Some idiot
keeps ringing
my doorbell
then running
away.
Is it you?

Man in No 3
(down hall).

Hehyheh
hehheh
heh!

October

11 Monday

Highbury District Council (Adult Ed. Dept.)
Council Offices
Highbury, London N10

Dear Mr Bean

I am writing on what I know is a very sensitive subject, but I hope you will appreciate my honesty and frankness.

You have been a most enthusiastic pupil at my poetry class, never failing to do your homework and always handing in on time the work which I have requested. I am afraid that I have to tell you, however, that there is something about your work which is really quite shocking, not only to myself, but also to your classmates. They are forced to bear witness to your poetry, as you always insist on reading it out loud during the class, banging the lid of your desk enthusiastically as you do so. As I cannot emphasise enough, we have nothing but admiration for your enthusiasm. But we have had complaints. You may remember that Ann Warburton was physically sick during your stirring rendition of your poem on the same subject (Vomiting), and has never returned. Dear old Derek didn't sleep for a week after the blood-letting trilogy. The class is now half the size it was at the beginning of term, and I'm sorry to say that you and your poetry are the chief cause of the decline in numbers.

Might we interest you in another subject? The Adult Education Institute has over a hundred courses running in the '93-'94 academic year and I am sure we could find one more attuned to your inclinations and enthusiasm. Car maintenance? Italian? I'm sure we could find you something. If you choose to leave our poetry class, we would naturally refund your course fee in full, and also pay the new course's fees for a full five years.

Yours sincerely

Rosemary Hosebury

Rosemary Hosebury (Ms)

Yah boo hiss

*I'm Mr. Dam Bean
Not Mr. Has Bean*

12 Tuesday

*As you might have guessed
You've made me depressed,*

10.15. Buy bottle of alcohol in shop

October

13 Wednesday

I can do rhymes
Time after time (s)

Whiskey is lovely

French Foreign Legion
010 33 4392 0047

BlaBlaBla

TEA -CHERS

7.30 Poetry Class

14 Thursday

Ring itma

Shirley where are you?
Shirley you don't understand

More Gobble Wobble

Wicky

October

15 Friday

Do everything extremely quietly don't make any noise at all I think
this might be what they call a hangover I've read about it in books
move very slowly and speak very very softly do not go out close
curtains sssssssssssssshhhhh ssssssssssssshhh sss ss ss ss shhh

16 Saturday

9.30 Go out quietly
      Shopping: Bread
                Ear plugs

12.00 Come in so, so quietly
       Tip toe up stairs

       SSSSShhh

17 Sunday

11.15 Don't go to church

October

18 Monday

4.15 Lemon

19 Tuesday

8.40 CAR RETURNED
YIPPEE!

God bless the Highland Police
Who returned my car
With its Reyssse (still in it)

2.10 Put music system in car
(needs new stylus)

Records for car: The Very Best of Shirley Bassey
Shirley at her Best
Best of Bassey
Bassey's Best of the Bestest

October

MICK'S KENDO CLUB

School Hall, 8.15
Wednesday Evening

Shops: Broom Handles
White sheet

7.30 Poetry Class
8.15 Kendo Class

Motor Show - Earl's Court

HOW TO GET THERE ON TIME

UURRRMMM URRRMM VRMMM

IGNORE TRAFFIC LIGHTS

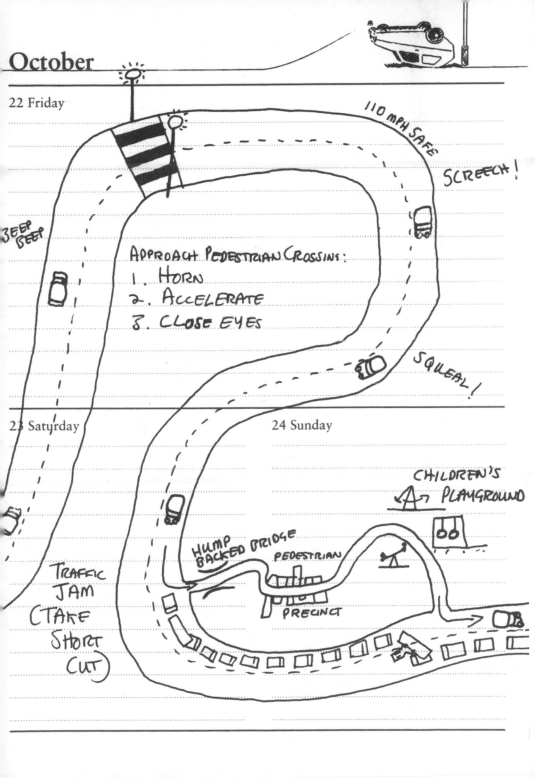

October

22 Friday

23 Saturday

24 Sunday

110 MPH SAFE

SCREECH!

JEEP BEEP

APPROACH PEDESTRIAN CROSSING:
1. HORN
2. ACCELERATE
3. CLOSE EYES

SQUEAL!

CHILDREN'S PLAYGROUND

TRAFFIC JAM (TAKE SHORT CUT)

HUMP BACKED BRIDGE

PEDESTRIAN PRECINCT

October

25 Monday

Petrol
Lettuce
Stamps

I thought girls
Always had curls

HAY
STACK →

85 mph SAFE

26 Tuesday

WET ROAD:
1. ACCELERATE
2. SWERVE FROM
   SIDE TO SIDE

ROUNDABOUT:
GO ROUND 3 TIMES
FLAT OUT

27 Wednesday

ROAD NARROWS

RELIANT ROBIN

WARP SPEED

POLICE ← CAR

NA NUR NA NUR

OUT

8.15 Kendo Class

28 Thursday

Plan: 8.15 Go to Japan

12.30 Have lunch

Not possible

4.00 Come home

October

29 Friday

NA NUR NA NUR

Shhhhhhh...

HIDE!

← N.B. Lost Police Car

30 Saturday

CAFÉ

POLICE TEA-BREAK

31 Sunday

MOTOR SHOW

SCCREEEECHH!

HooRAH!

November

1 Monday

Oven broken — Ring Gas Man

Buy salad stuff : Tomatoes
                  Cucumber
                  Weeds
                  Insects
                  Soil

Dinner: Salad & Bread

2 Tuesday

9.00 Gas Man

12.00 Oven still broken

Lunch: Salad

stupid STUPID
Gas Man

Dinner: Salad

November

I HATE SALAD

Gas Man

8.15: Try and cook without oven (Lamb chops)

9.00: FIRE BRIGADE

2.45am Sleep.

9.00 Shops: ~~Flour~~ Flour x 30 lbs
Eggs

Plot plot plot plot plot

November

5 Friday Guy Fawkes Night

Flipping dangerous (Flipper!) treason plot treason plot treason plot plot plot plot plot plot plot

8pm. Bonfire Party (in Park)

GET THEM WITH FLOUR BOMB
(then throw eggs)
if time

6 Saturday

9.00 Police station
Questioning

all day

7 Sunday

Fireworks Fright

POLICE WERE CALLED to a bonfire party last night where a man was apprehended under suspicion of intending to plant a large explosive on the bonfire. "What we suspected of being a large bomb turned out to be a bag of flour and eggs", said event organiser Don Haze. "When I dragged him out of the tree he told me he was just about to make a cake."

Mr Bean, of Arbor Road, London, was detained at local

November

8 Monday

VROOM!
VROOM!

ALL THE SMOKERS IN THE WORLD.

"COMMON SENSE"

© Mr. Bean

9 Tuesday

1.00 Egg

7.00 Another egg

METROPOLITAN POLICE
RECEIPT

your ref:

our ref:

Surrendered Goods

2 BROOM HANDLES

P.C.R.Leans

The above items have been confiscated pending
a decision by local magistrates

8.15
Mickes Kendo Club

Challenge Mick
to DUEL

5.15 Duel at Dawn

Requirements: Broom handle
Sheet

Report: 4.45 Hospital (neck brace)
6.00 Police (re. broom handles)

November

12 Friday

4.15 Stake out

WHAT!?!

Plan

13 Saturday   14 Sunday

LIBRARY

PARK

BEAN WITH
BIG STICK

BUSH

AMBUSH

HIT! HIT!
HIT!

Usual route
of G. Gummer

GET
AWAY

MINI

November

15 Monday

SHIRLEY BASSEY LETTER

ʊ. ʊ. ʊ. ʊ. ʊ. ʊ. ʊ. ʊ. ʊ. ʊ. ʊ. ʊ. ʊ. important

4.10 POST BOX

16 Tuesday

If I was going to choose a day
I would choose Choose-day.

4.07 Gummer Ambush   POLICE SUSPICIOUS

HIDE DIARY

GUMMER 2

STRETCH   TUG

November

17 Wednesday

HIDE DIARY

12.15 POLICE CALLING ROUND.

8.15 Advanced Knodr Club
N.B. COUNTRY DANCING meet Monday

18 Thursday

TOAST RECIPE

Burn Bread
Eat

19 Friday

Shirley Bassey
Entertainments

Las Vegas • Hollywood • Monte Carlo • London

Mr Bean
c/o Mrs Wickets
"Daffodils"
Room 2
12 Arbor Road
London N10

Dear Mr Bean

Thank you for your recent letter to Ms Bassey: I'm sorry I've been so late in replying.

I am sorry to say that the vocal microphones used by Ms Bassey during her performances are extremely expensive items, and it would be impossible to send them as souvenirs to fans who request them.

Enclosed is a signed photograph as partial compensation!

Yours sincerely

Richard Kershaw

Richard Kershaw
Technical Manager
Shirley Bassey Ents.

Write again

November

22 Monday

START→

1 — 2 Tum TeeTum Tra la la

7.00 Country Dancing

23 Tuesday

Jump

AIRBORNE

TWIST

(Tum) Tra la-la -te tum tum tiddle tiddle

November

24 Wednesday

Boff   Boff

Dum   Bang
      Bang

Titty

Trrrrummm

Deedee
Deedee
Dee

Vooop!

25 Thursday

Hop

Skip

La —la —la

teedly — dee   Bink   Bink   Boodle   Baff

FINISH

November

2.00
Shoes
Honey

Shirley Bassey
Entertainments

Las Vegas · Hollywood · Monte Carlo · London

Mr Bean
c/o Mrs Wickets
"Daffodils"
Room 2
12 Arbor Road
London N10

Dear Mr Bean

I acknowledge receipt of your letter of the 17th of July.

I understand that we misread the request in your last letter, and that
there was no grammatical error. Your request was to BE one of Ms
Bassey's microphones, rather than to posses one.

I should warn you that, in accordance with the policy of this office,
your letter has been passed to the police.

Yours sincerely

Adrian Silverman

Adrian Silverman
for Shirley Bassey Ents.

November

29 Monday <u>Mrs. Wicket going to Bournemouth</u>

Look after Kipper

KIPPER

Please look after
Kipper. He is
very sensitive and
needs feeding
<u>every day</u>
Mrs Wicket

7.00
Country Dancing
Tra-la-la-dee-dum-te-tum

1-2 1-2 1-2 1-2 and rest.

25 days to Christmas

December

No 3.

Dear Mr Bean,
Have you heard
that barking from
Mrs Wicket's?

Man in No 3.
(down hall).

It is you that's
barking!

Nagging thought

2 Thursday

Nagging thought

December

3 Friday

Nagging thought

4 Saturday

8.00 Nagging tho~~t~~

oh my God NO
AAAARGHH

12 MIDNIGHT: Put Kipper's
corpse in middle of road
(Act Natural)

5 Sunday

MRS. WICKET BACK
FROM BOURNEMOUTH

Dear ~~Mrs~~ Mrs. Wicket
I was so sorry to hear that
Kipper had escaped and been run
over while my back was turned.
I think I was ironing at the time,
~~but~~ although I did hear brakes
and, thinking it was a bat screeching
sub-sonically, ~~I~~

December

6 Monday

MADAME
SANDRA

Fortunes Told
Racing Tips
Contact the Dead!
081 524 5501

11am Funeral (Kipper)

THINKS ←

1.15 Sink blocked

7 Tuesday

Ring Madame Sandra

2.00 Madame Sandra

No luck

December

11.00 Madame Sandra
(Some progress)

Mum's
ghost?

Madame Sandra

11.45 Madame Sandra

MADE CONTACT WITH Mum

Question: Where is the plunger for the sink?

Answer: Under the stairs

12.10 Unblock sink ✓

December

10 Friday

1.00 Crisps

11 Saturday

2 weeks till
Chrizzy

12 Sunday

ALL IN ONE STUMPS
© Mr. Bean

December

13 Monday

9.15 Madame Sandra
(Talk to Charles Dickens)

Q: What was supposed to happen to Edwin Drood?

A: Hadn't made up his mind.

14 Tuesday

Dear ~~Santa~~ Mr. Claus, ← more respectful
I hope you are well. I am fine.
There really is not very long to go now until Christmas, so I
thought I might write ~~and~~ with a provisional list of presents
~~in order of preference~~:

1. A quantity of High Explosive
   (Semtex, or equivalent)
2. Small rubber fork.
3. New mother
4. Brass hook (Toilet door)
5. t.b.a.

December

15 Wednesday

10.00 Buy New TV

+ Radio Times
TV Times
~~Financial Times~~
TV Quick

QUICK!

16 Thursday

NEW ROOM PLANS FOR CHRISTMAS
(TO ACCOMODATE TV)

DOOR

WINDOW   TV

BED

WINDOW

CHAIR

December

17 Friday

CHAIR

DOOR

WINDOW

(LOTS OF SPACE)

WINDOW

BED

---

18 Saturday   **19 Sunday**

1 Week till

Chrizzzy

TV

BRACKET

CHAIR

DOOR

(EVEN MORE SPACE)

BED

December

20 Monday

BED

DOOR

WINDOW

CHAIR

(MOST SPACE)

TV

21 Tuesday

("Daffodils")

Dear Mr. Claus

I hope you are well. I am fine. Only four days till the birthday of our Lord Jesus Christ, and I've had a change of heart: I would now like a Drum kit which I can bash and bash and bash

New order
1. Snare drum
2. Cymbal
3. Bass drum
4. Tom-Tom
4a. Hi-hat

5. Tom-Tom
6. " "
7. " "
8. Brass hook (TOILET DOOR)
9.

22. Santas

December

22 Wednesday

POST LETTER TO SANTA

DRUM PRACTICE:

Right hand	Tink	Tink	Tink	Tink	Tink	Tink	Tink	Tink	Tink	Tink
Left hand		Chap		Chap		Chap		Chap		Chap
Right Foot	Boom		BoomBoom		Boom		BoomBoom		Boom	
Left Foot				Chish				Chish		

23 Thursday

Santa should get letter ~~this letter~~ this morning

Try: Biddley Biddley Biddley
L R L   R L R   L R L

Biddley phoomp titty
L R L   F   R R

Bash bash
L   L

EXCITING EXCITING EXCITING EXCITING EXCITING

If I get a drum kit
I'm going to go mad

December

24 Friday

I want a drum kit
I want a drum kit
Tiddle diddle rapple rapple
Bum Boom tish.

Shops: Buy cracker

Buy brass hook.

25 Saturday   Christmas Day

26 Sunday

OOOh! BRASS HOOK for Christmas!

Just what I NEED!!

My present

No other presents

(Cracker didn't crack - send back to man)

December

27 Monday   Boxing Day

10.00 Go to Park   (empty)

No shops open

Practise on
drum kit

Evening: stay in

28 Tuesday

Water plant   (in next door garden)

Practise on drum
kit

I don't like Christmas very much if I had to be honest

December

Practise on drum kit

Shops: Bread
Hazelnut
Tangerine?

9.00 Bird Watching

COMMON WADER

BACK

FRONT

TAKING OFF

SIDE

IN FLIGHT

7.00 Common Wader
(Gas Mark 7
2-2½ hrs.)

December/January

31 Friday

New Year Resolutions

1.
2.
3. Tidy room
4.

Marriage

Can't think of anything

1 Saturday

BRAND new YEAR
clean and sparkling and shiney
1994
GLEAM
SPARKLE

2 Sunday

Nº 3.

Dear Mr Bean,
Would you
like to pop round
for a New Year
drink sometime?

Martin Davis.
(Man in Nº 3.)

P.T.O ⟹

1994 Year Planner

	January	February	March	April	May	June
Mon						
Tue		1	1			
Wed		2	2			1
Thu		3				2
Fri		4				3
Sat	1					4
Sun	2				1	5
Mon	3*				2*	6*
Tue	4*				3	7
Wed	5				4	8
Thu	6				5	9
Fri	7				6	10
Sat	8				7	11
Sun	9				8	12
Mon	10				9	13
Tue	11				10	14
Wed	12				11	15
Thu	13				12	16
Fri	14					17
Sat	15					18
Sun	16				15	19
Mon	17			18	16	20
Tue	18	22		19	17	21
Wed	19	23	23	20	18	22
Thu	20	24	24	21	19	23
Fri	21	25	25	22	20	24
Sat	22	26	26	23	21	25
Sun	23	27	27	24	22	26
Mon	24	28	28	25	23	27
Tue	25		29	26	24	28
Wed	26		30	27	25	29
Thu	27		31	28	26	30
Fri	28			29	27	
Sat	29			30	28	
Sun	30				29	
Mon	31				30*	
Tue					31	

BURY HATCHET

January	February	March	April	May	June
3 UK, R of Ireland		17 Ireland (N & R)	1 UK, R of Irelland	2 UK	6 R of Ireland
4 Scotland			4 England, Ireland	30 UK	
			(N & R), Wales		

1994 Year Planner

	July	August	September	October	November	December
Mon		1*				
Tue		2			1	
Wed		3			2	
Thu		4	1		3	1
Fri	1	5	2		4	2
Sat	2	6	3	1	5	3
Sun	3	7	4	2	6	4
Mon	4	8	5	3	7	5
Tue	5	9	6	4	8	6
Wed	6	10	7	5	9	7
Thu	7	11	8	6	10	8
Fri	8	12	9	7	11	9
Sat	9	13	10	8	12	10
Sun	10	14	11	9	13	11
Mon	11	15	12	10	14	12
Tue	12*	16	13	11	15	13
Wed	13	17	14	12	16	14
Thu	14	18	15	13	17	15
Fri	15	19	16	14	18	16
Sat	16	20	17 *10.00 Sex Change?*	15	19	17
Sun	17	21	18 *(Dr. Lahota)*	16	20	18
Mon	18	22	19	17	21	19
Tue	19	23	20	18	22	20
Wed	20	24	21	19	23	21
Thu	21	25	22	20	24	22
Fri	22	26	23	21	25	23
Sat	23	27	24	22	26	24
Sun	24	28	25	23	27	25
Mon	25	29*	26	24	28	26*
Tue	26	30	27	25	29	27*
Wed	27	31	28	26	30	28
Thu	28		29	27		29
Fri	29		30	28		30
Sat	30			29		31
Sun	31			30		
Mon				31*		
Tue						
	July	August	September	October	November	December

12 N Ireland	1 R of Ireland, Scotland 29 England, N Ireland Wales	3 R of Ireland		26 UK, R of Ireland 27 UK, R of Ireland

← CLUE.

HANGMAN

Notes

? ? ?

HAT x
COT x
PAT ↑
MOT x
TOM ↑
TAM x
SAP ↑
LAP ↑
NAP ↑
TAP ↑
NAP x
LAP ↑
RAT ↑
NUT ↑
PUT x
MUT x
ROP ↑
COP ↑

PIT x NO
SOP x
SOAP NO
TOP x
MOP x
LOP x
HOP x
HELP
NAP x
MIT ↑
MAT ↑
CAT

Chadwell School for Boys

Term: SUMMER TERM, 1971 Name: SEAN

Subject	Mark	Comments	
History	35%	He has no sense of history. But then, of course, he has no sense.	T.A.P.R.
Chemistry	53%	He is inventive. As a result, form 5B is lucky to be alive.	T.A.B.
Mathematics	94%	An obnoxious, self-satisfied, self-centred, shabby, dribbling, bone-idle, toadying cow-pat of a pupil; his most revolting quality being that he is quite, quite brilliant.	M.J.L.
Physics	65%	Very encouraging. A boy died when co-operating with his lie-detector experiment, as you know, but nevertheless the exam results are excellent.	Mr Hutt
Geography	54%	A surprisingly good result considering he only succeeded in finding the classroom twice this term.	K.W.
Biology	41%	He really has no idea, but then hopefully he will never breed.	P.A.B.
Religious knowledge	25%	No progress this year, sadly. He once claimed that he worshipped the God of Lemonade, which rather confused us all, I'm afraid.	N.N.
Art	58%	He draws well, but has difficulty with nudes (looking at them).	P.B.

Good luck. He'll need it. S Love

Headmaster

© Mr. Bean 1993

Notes

PLAN

→ 1. Photocopy this × 10 million

(Joanis Copyshop
105lip St.)

than 2.

it.

Graph

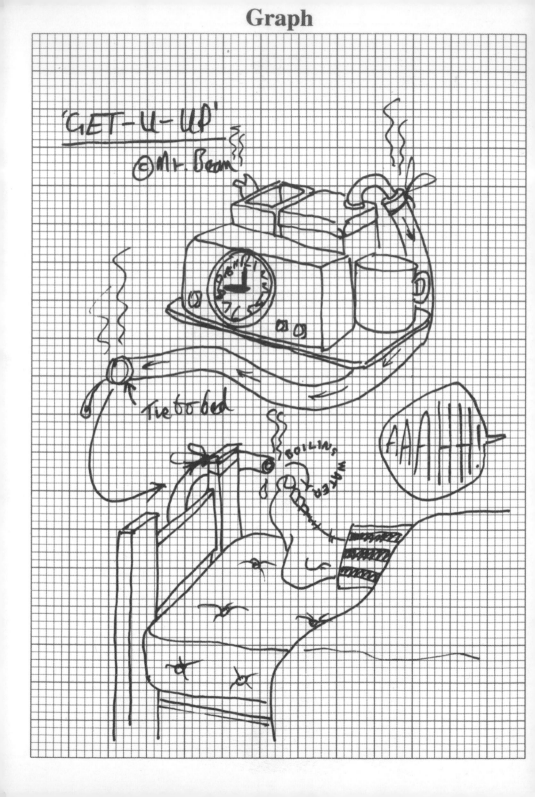

Graph